THE ASSASSINATION OF THE ARCHBISHOP

Thomas Becket and the European Stage

WILLIAM MOYLE

BOOKBORN PUBLICATIONS

2018

This book is dedicated to the congregation of the Church of St. Thomas à Becket, Huntington, Herefordshire. It comes with love and thanks for their continued kindness and companionship to the author and his wife.

THE ASSASSINATION
OF THE ARCHBISHOP
by William Moyle

Text © William Moyle, 2018
Copyright © Bookborn Publications, 2018

ISBN 978 0 9957008 2 6

Bookborn Publications
info@bookborn.co.uk

Printed in the UK

CONTENTS

1

THE HISTORICAL BACKGROUND

There was a time when every well educated British schoolboy and girl, asked to name seminal episodes in their country's history, could narrate how King Alfred burnt the cakes, nominate the encounter between Robert Bruce and the spider, describe the death of Lord Nelson with the loyal Captain Hardy kissing farewell to his much loved commander, and relate the gory assassination of Thomas Becket in Canterbury cathedral.

The case of Becket sits comfortably within the British historical tradition of venerating premature death or glorious failure. One thinks of Wolfe expiring on the Heights of Abraham, Sir John Moore dying of his wounds at Corunna, the fate of Scott and his companions in the Antarctic, overcome by cold and overwhelmed by grief at their failure to precede Amundsen to the South Pole, and the tragic disappearance of Mallory and Irvine on Mount Everest. All of these episodes in British history may well have given rise to myths, embellishments and distortions but nevertheless the delicate romanticism attaching to the gallant loser, or a brilliant future destroyed in embryo, has a unique appeal to the British personality.

Thus Becket's murder has a dual fascination for readers of history in that it marked both the cutting down of a great and powerful figure in his full manhood, a colossus of his time, and that this was executed in the most sacred of sanctums. Equally, in order to understand the course of events and their consequences it is necessary for the historian to study both the personal life of Becket himself and the European stage upon which he moved since its principal performers had a profound impact on this remarkable story.

For many years throughout medieval Europe there prevailed a savage and unremitting struggle for primacy between the pontiff and the Holy Roman Emperor. Over decades European secular rulers had gradually expanded and developed their fiefdoms to such an extent and also demonstrated such dangerous tendencies towards spiritual independence, that Rome feared for the primacy of the papacy. It was therefore determined to assert its divine right to obedience from its flock. All men and women, however elevated in rank, were to submit to the supremacy of the church in both spiritual and secular matters, since priests were God's agents on earth and thus superior to any monarch, however powerful.

This assertion had been initiated in 1075 under the leadership of the former Cardinal Hildebrand, who became Pope Gregory VII (1073–1085), and was continued by his successors. However the monarchs, while enjoying absolute power within their own kingdoms, and experiencing evermore freedom from Rome, were not inclined to submit to the papal reform movement. Friction sparked military hostilities between the papacy and the Holy Roman Emperor Frederick I (1152–1190), 'Barbarossa' (so-called because of his red beard), and the issue was always: "Which was supreme, Pope or Emperor?" [1]

In particular, the Holy Roman Emperors before Frederick I had continued to exercise their perceived right to appoint church officials, including the investiture of bishops, and the Papacy's resistance to this led to the Investiture Contest in which for decades there were excommunications by one side and depositions by the other, with successive diplomatic and military encounters between both. These encouraged internal violence throughout much of Germany until exhaustion persuaded the parties to meet near the Rhineland city of Worms in 1122.

Here the Emperor Henry V and the pope Calixtus II compromised over the investiture of bishops in that henceforth cathedral canons were to elect the bishop who would in future receive the ring and crosier (the spiritual symbols of his office) from his ecclesiastical superior while, as symbol of the bishop-elect's temporal powers (which the pope recognised as emanating from the emperor), the sceptre would be transferred by the emperor or his representative. In addition, within Germany, the emperor or his representative would have the right to attend elections and resolve any disputes between the candidates; which meant in effect a de facto veto. In the Empire outside Germany (e.g. Italy and Burgundy) there would be no right of attendance by the Emperor and, furthermore, the conferring of spiritual power would precede that of temporal, with the transfer of the sceptre following within six months.

This compromise, known as the Concordat of Worms, largely resolved the Investiture Contest although subsequently the Emperor Frederick I endeavoured to interfere with the process.

The Holy Roman Empire is one of the great paradoxes of European history. As Voltaire wrote in 1756: "This agglomeration which was called and still calls itself the Holy Roman Empire was neither holy, nor Roman, nor an empire", and indeed for much of its existence was an empire more theoretical than substantial; and yet it survived for a thousand years. It was conceived by the papacy out of the wreckage of the old Roman empire which, by the fourth century, had fractured into the Eastern and Western Empires before the latter collapsed a hundred years later, while the Eastern Empire in its Byzantine form survived for nearly ten centuries.

In the face of chaos and barbarism from which they felt threatened, following the sacking of Rome in 410,[2] a succession of popes wished to restore the Western Empire in order to secure the church's position, with the empire acting as its guardian, while at the same time neutralising the Byzantines with whom the papacy had substantial doctrinal differences. By the eighth century AD the dominant European power was the kingdom of the Franks whose frontiers stretched from Brittany to the Elbe and from Hamburg to central Italy. Upon this kingdom and its rulers the papacy determined to grant imperial status. Thus it was that in Rome on the 25th December 800

Pope Leo III crowned Charlemagne, the greatest of the Carolingian kings, emperor of the new Roman Empire.

Following the deaths of Charlemagne in 814 and his son Louis in 840, the Frankish empire splintered, and from the eastern portion there evolved the kingdom of Germany whose monarchs were traditionally chosen by election. During the course of the following centuries the precedents were established whereby the German king almost always became the Holy Roman emperor by process of election.

In December 1356 the Emperor Charles IV published his Golden Bull which provided for an electoral college of seven who were the archbishops of Trier, Mainz and Cologne, the Duke of Saxony known as the Elector of Saxony, the Count Palatine of the Rhine, known as the Elector Palatine, the Margrave of Brandenburg known as the Elector of Brandenburg, and the King of Bohemia.

By the middle of the 16th century, and with the Reformation now maturing, the electors of Saxony, Brandenburg and the Palatine had become Protestants while the king of Bohemia and the spiritual electors of Trier, Mainz and Cologne remained Catholics.

In 1623 the Elector Palatine, Frederick V, was stripped of his office for his involvement with the revolt in Bohemia which triggered the Thirty Years War, and his electorate was given to the Duke of Bavaria, Maximilian I, who became known as the Elector of Bavaria. In the Peace of Westphalia, 1648, the office of Elector Palatine was restored to Frederick's son, Charles Louis, but as a new Electorate (i.e. the holder lost precedence) while at the same time the Electorate of Bavaria was confirmed. The eight electors were increased to nine in 1692 when a new electorate was created for the Duke of Brunswick-Luneburg who became known as the Elector of Hanover.

Elections were held in Frankfurt cathedral as were imperial coronations from 1562; the last emperor to be crowned by the pope in Rome was Frederick III in 1452.

The Imperial Diet or general assembly of the Holy Roman Empire emerged over the centuries and met in different cities throughout the Empire until in 1663 the Perpetual Diet was established at

Regensburg. The Diet was an assembly of the various estates of the Empire represented by three colleges being the Electoral College, the College of Imperial Princes and that of Imperial Cities. The power of the Diet in relation to the Emperor gradually increased, until it was enshrined in the Peace of Westphalia, 1648, which bound the emperor to accept all decisions made by the Diet.

Two dynasties dominated the empire during the 12th and 13th centuries: the Hohenstaufen, a powerful Swabian family, named after the castle of Staufen in north-east Swabia, whose members provided emperors from 1138 to 1254, and the Welfs, (or Wuelps) a Frankish family with lands in Saxony and Bavaria and one of whom, Otto IV was emperor from 1198 to 1214.

The politics of Germany and Italy were partly driven throughout this period by a rift between the two families which emanated from thwarted Hohenstaufen expectations on the death of Henry V in 1125. The Swabian family thought Frederick of Swabia, closely related as he was to the late emperor, would be elected as his successor. Instead Lothair of Supplinburg, a friend of the Welfs, (and eventually connected to them by marriage) was chosen. Such choice was followed by civil war; a conflict which raged through central Germany until the election of Frederick I Barbarossa in 1152, since he was the son of a Welf mother and a Hohenstaufen father. Frederick by charm and diplomacy appeased the Saxon dynasty and good relations were restored, temporarily.

However the emperor's numerous attempts to assert his authority in Italy eventually brought him into conflict with both the papacy and the Welfs and led to proxy wars which persisted through the 13th and 14th centuries. The surrogate Italian protagonists were the Guelfs (or Guelphs)[3] and the Ghibellines; the latter being the party of the emperor and aristocracy while the Guelfs were the papal and popular party. Central Italy and large cities with a tradition of independence tended to be Guelf while Northern Italy and the nobility favoured the Ghibellines.

The Welf and Hohenstaufen dynasties were ultimately reconciled when in 1235 Frederick II (a Hohenstaufen) granted the Duchy of

Brunswick-Luneburg to Otto the Child, also known as Otto I, a Welf and grandson of Henry the Lion, Duke of Saxony. He was a nephew of the deposed and late Emperor Otto IV. His father was William of Winchester, the youngest son of Henry the Lion.

2

THE PROTAGONISTS

During Becket's years in public life (1155–1170) the European theatre was dominated by five protagonists: the Emperor, the Pope, Louis VII of France, the English king, Henry II, and his wife, Eleanor of Aquitaine; at least three of whom dignify Carlyle's dictum that "As I take it, Universal History, the history of what man has accomplished in this world, is at bottom the History of the Great Men who have worked here".[4]

On the major issue of primacy during this period England tended to support the emperor while France aligned herself with the pontiff. Within this supreme and continuing struggle there was further hostility between England and France over English territorial claims to substantial sectors of the French lands. Furthermore both the empire and the papacy had bitter internal disputes which in each case threatened their very existence.

THE HOLY ROMAN EMPEROR

Becket's public career coincided with Frederick I's rule as Holy Roman Emperor since Frederick was crowned in Rome in June 1155 by Pope Hadrian IV.[5]

Distinctive with his auburn beard, penetrating eyes and genial countenance, a man of enormous energy, the new emperor was a polymath displaying considerable military skills, administrative ability and a dazzling personality who demanded, and received, fierce loyalty from his followers. He was to become the towering figure in twelfth century Europe: "No German sovereign since Charlemagne possessed qualities so well fitted for the governance of the German people. He could both frighten and charm. Churchmen, nobles, peasants were prepared to regard him as the perfect knight". [Fisher]

Germany consisted of more than 1600 states, many minute, while a few such as Bavaria, Swabia and Saxony were substantial. Throughout his reign the Emperor dealt with squabbling territories: Principalities, Duchies, Counties, Margravates,[6] Landgraviates, Archbishoprics, Bishoprics and Free Cities, and with their bickering princelings and other rulers, using firmness tempered with diplomacy and exercising all his considerable conciliatory powers.

However, at his succession in 1155 he was confronted by three threats to his supremacy. The first, with which he speedily dealt, was that posed by his powerful and ambitious Welf cousin, Henry the Lion (1129–80),[7] whose late father, Henry the Proud, had been stripped of the duchies of Saxony[8] and Bavaria in 1138 by Frederick's predecessor Conrad III. Barbarossa recognising his cousin as potentially a major source of opposition within Germany, restored Bavaria to Henry thus assuaging the movement towards internal state nationalism.[9]

The other two threats, which proved to be intractable, were from Frederick's Italian dominions and the papacy. The emperor was determined to stamp imperial authority on northern Italy, not least because he saw wealthy commercial cities like Milan, Brescia, Florence, Spoleto and Verona as promising lucrative sources of revenue from imperial taxes.

In the course of his reign Frederick undertook seven expeditions south of the Alps. During the first of these, as we have seen, pope Adrian IV (the 'English' pope) crowned Barbarossa Roman Emperor[10] in Rome on 18th June 1155. His subsequent campaigns produced mixed fortunes partly because of the Lombard League.

The League was a coalition of city communes formed in 1167[11] to resist the attempts by the Hohenstaufen emperors to assert their hegemony over Italy, an authority which Barbarossa had proclaimed at the Imperial Diet of Roncaglia (near Piacenza) in November 1158 where four eminent jurists from Bologna were asked to determine the rights of the parties. Their decision confirmed the emperor's claims and his sovereignty by divine right; a ruling which was not accepted by the League.

Furthermore the Emperor's campaigns were interrupted by the need to return to Germany and settle internal disputes and his early military successes in Italy were followed by reverses, culminating in the severe defeat at the battle of Legnano near Milan in May 1176. Frederick eventually recognised the folly of continuing hostilities and the parties agreed a truce at the Peace of Venice in 1178. In due course this led to a permanent settlement at the Peace of Constance in 1183, whereby, in return for the League recognising the Emperor's nominal authority in Italy, he accepted the right of the northern cities to substantial devolution of power.

The League, however, subsisted until the death of Frederick II, the last Hohenstaufen emperor, in 1250, following which it was dissolved.

Initially Barbarossa's relationship with the papacy had been warm and, by the Treaty of Constance in March 1153, the emperor had agreed that in return for the Pope, Eugenius III, crowning him as such [12] he would defend the Lateran against its enemies and in particular Roger of Sicily. [13] Also he would help the pope recover Rome, the control of which had been lost in 1143 when Roman rebels declared a republic and the then pope, Innocent II, was virtually stripped of authority. In 1155 German arms recovered Rome for the Lateran, while in April of that year Frederick was crowned king of Italy in Pavia before the supreme crowning as Roman Emperor in Rome. This act by Pope Adrian IV marked the high tide of friendship between the Empire and the Papacy.

However the waters of mutual regard ebbed swiftly when in 1159 Adrian died and a majority of the cardinals elected Cardinal Roland to succeed him as Alexander III. Alexander was a firm protagonist of the Hildebrand doctrine of papal primacy in the Investiture Contest and the remaining cardinals, seeking perhaps to appease the Emperor, favoured Cardinal Octavian, a man with imperial leanings, and he, taking the name Victor IV, was elected by them as the anti-pope. Neither man was able to assert supremacy in Rome and in this somewhat unsatisfactory situation both parties solicited the Emperor's support. Frederick responded by summoning a synod to convene at Pavia in Lombardy in February 1160 to resolve the issue. Alexander III refused to attend and in his absence the synod declared Victor IV to be the legitimate pope.

Alexander's riposte was to excommunicate the emperor. But while most countries initially recognised Victor IV as pope a significant development ensued on 23rd September 1162 at Coucy-Sur-Loire where Alexander, who had been living in exile, met Louis VII of France and Henry II of England and both monarchs formally recognised him as the legitimate pope.

Following the Emperor's defeat at Legnano in May 1176 he realised the futility of further hostilities with the papacy, and by the Peace of Agnani in October of that year he formally recognised Alexander III as pope, a recognition which led to the formal reconciliation of emperor and pope in the Treaty of Venice in July 1177.

THE POPE

As mentioned already, the Emperor was not alone in confronting internal unrest which threatened his own position and it has been seen that the papacy also was riven by disputes over leadership elections and the struggle for power. On numerous occasions during the twelfth century, the church of Rome was led simultaneously by at least two men claiming to be the legitimately elected pope. This was despite the fact that in 1059 Pope Nicholas II had decreed that the cardinals alone had the right to elect a pope. However, it had not been made clear in the decree as to the precise roles in the election which were to be played by the cardinal – bishops (whose participation was paramount) and that of the cardinal – priests and deacons (who were envisaged to be primarily counsellors).

The effect of this was that, for decades following Pope Nicholas's decree and throughout much of the twelfth century, many papal elections produced a majority for one candidate and substantial support for another, with the result that each side claimed legitimate victory, thus giving rise to the age of the pope and anti-pope. [14] Frequently the cardinals voted for whichever candidate they considered to be either for or against the imperial interest, as the case might be, such was the interlocking of imperial politics and papal affairs.

The electoral issue was finally resolved by the Third Lateran Council in 1179 which, led by pope Alexander III, determined that all future elections would require a two thirds majority of those cardinals voting, for a candidate to be successful. [15]

It can be seen, therefore that the pope was largely dependant on other European rulers for the security of his position.

In fact the pontiff's vulnerability is further demonstrated by the fact that between 1095 and 1165 seven popes lost control and their position in Rome and sought protection in France. [16]

Therefore it was not surprising that for most of this period the French monarch and the pope enjoyed a cordial relationship. There was, of course, a very good reason for France to embrace all the friends she could since her overwhelming consideration was the perceived menace of England.

THE KING OF FRANCE

The early Carpetian dynasty proved to be durable and for most of the 12th century France was governed by Louis VI ('The Fat', 1108–1137) and then by his son Louis VII (1137–1180). When the earlier Louis came to the French throne the monarchy had control only over the Isle de France since major fiefdoms such as Burgundy, Toulouse, Aquitaine and Champagne were merely nominally in suzerainty to the French crown.

Louis VI was determined to cement his position on the Isle de France by taming his recalcitrant barons and thereafter pursuing a policy of expansion; a course which led him into conflict with Henry I of England whose Duchy of Normandy was pressing upon the French king's northern border. Henry had seized the strategically important castle of Gisors,[17] in breach of an earlier agreement with Louis that it should remain neutral and so precipitated hostilities which continued for most of the years of Louis's rule.

In 1120 Louis appealed to Pope Calixtus II to help the cause of peace and the pope met Henry at Gisors but conceded the latter's right to retain the fortress.

While for the most part Louis was careful and shrewd, his son, who succeeded to the throne in 1137, was delightful, charming, pious and somewhat inert. Unlike his father, who had been a man of action, Louis VII relied upon diplomacy and the support of the church in his struggles with the English. In 1159 the king of France supported Pope Alexander III against the imperial anti-pope, so further cementing the relationship between Paris and Rome.

Louis married Eleanor, Duchess of Aquitaine, on 25th July 1137 but, some fifteen years later, in one of the most extraordinary errors of political judgment in French medieval history, he initiated the annulment of the marriage which was effected on the 21st March 1152. Eleanor had brought to their union the great estates of Guienne, Auvergne and Aquitaine which were now lost to the French crown.

HENRY II

Shortly after the annulment, on the 18th May 1152, Eleanor married Henry Plantagenet Count of Anjou, upon which event the control of Aquitaine and most of South-west France passed to the man shortly to become Henry II of England.

Henry was crowned king on 19th December 1154 and came to the English throne as the founder of the Plantagenet dynasty which was destined to rule England until bloodily expunged on Bosworth Field over three hundred years later.[18]

At his accession Henry had the most extensive dominions and the greatest power of any twelfth century European monarch. Here was a most remarkable man already glowing in the admiration and envy of all Europe for his outstanding military talent in clearing his Normandy Duchy of invaders and rebellious barons and then stamping his authority on his English inheritance. The extent of his domains was vast, stretching as it did from the Cheviot Hills to the mountains of Spain.

The new king was good-looking with a thickset frame of medium height and a bull neck surmounted by close-cropped red hair. [19] A linguist, he was intelligent, energetic, able, capricious and impatient and being quick tempered, he inherited the tradition of Angevin rages. This was a man of action with astonishing reserves of mental and physical stamina and who was both ruthless and passionate.

He led a peripatetic court constantly traversing the hills and valleys of his great dominions; administering justice, centralising government, [20] reforming finances, subduing malcontents in Anjou or rebellious burghers in Toulouse, while claiming and receiving fealty over all the British Isles. He was as accessible to the humblest citizen as to a baron with great estates and despite his myriad public commitments, Henry's prodigious energy enabled him to demonstrate and enjoy his skilful pursuit of both field sports and his female subjects.

His reign witnessed the establishment and application of English Common Law and assizes with trial by jury, while his imposition of scutage [21] in lieu of military service at a stroke provided a regular source of revenue for the king's government, enabled Henry to raise a force of mercenary troops and emasculated the power of the baronage.

Henry's foreign policy broadly followed that of his grandfather Henry I which consisted of open or concealed hostility to the French king while maintaining close relations with the Holy Roman Emperor. The earlier Henry in 1114 had arranged the marriage of his daughter Matilda to the Emperor Henry V thus establishing diplomatic friendship between the empire and England. Seven years later, in January 1121, the English king strengthened these relations by marrying, as his second wife, a German, Adeliza, daughter of the Duke of Lower Lorraine.

His grandson was no great friend of Rome through his boorish behaviour in church, lack of courtesy to the clergy and insistence upon the secular courts having sentencing jurisdiction over priests

17

found guilty of crimes by the church. Furthermore there was to be no right of appeal to the Papacy without the king's consent.

French and church hostility, family connections and pragmatism, combined to continue England's alliance with the Empire.

ELEANOR OF AQUITAINE

If Henry was a remarkable man, his wife, Eleanor (c1122–1204), was one of the outstanding personalities in medieval Europe: Duchess of Aquitaine and Countess of Poitou (1137–1204), Queen Consort of France (1137–1152) and of England (1154–1204), English Regent while her son Richard I fought in the Third Crusade, she had two children by her French husband and another eight by Henry. She was the mother of three kings (i.e. Henry 'the Young King,' crowned in 1170,[22] who died in 1183, Richard I and John), and two queens (Eleanor, Queen of Castile and Joan, Queen of Sicily), and was for decades at the very centre of power.

Eleanor was beautiful into old age, or rather described as *perpulchra* meaning very or more than beautiful. She was well educated, being proficient in arithmetic, Latin and history, music (a competent harpist) and literature, embroidery and needlepoint, while enjoying conversation, dancing and field sports.

A highly intelligent woman she charmed many whom she met, but by others was regarded as somewhat 'fast'. Like her English husband she was formidable, strong-minded, wilful and energetic. Such forceful personalities were almost bound to have a marriage both turbulent and fractious and so it proved to be.[23]

Eleanor was indeed intrepid as she had demonstrated when, as Duchess and leader of Aquitaine, insisting upon accompanying her first husband on the Second Crusade (1147–9). Inspired by the eloquent and impassioned preaching of Bernard, Abbot of Clairvaux, the German King Conrad III (1093–1152) and Louis both assembled substantial armies for the expedition.[24]

The French monarch left St-Denis on the 8th June 1147, and after meeting his followers in Metz a few days later, he and his army travelled via Worms and Mainz, where they crossed the Rhine and then through Bavaria to Ratisbon (Regensburg) which they reached on the 29th June. They then followed the Danube valley to Vienna before crossing the vast Hungarian plain and, turning south in Buda, they passed through Belgrade.

Reaching Branitz, the fringe of the Byzantine empire, by the end of August that great mass of people and animals crossed the Danube with the Carpathians frowning down from the north-east on an expedition with a dismal future. They continued south through Sofia and the Balkans in the early autumn and arrived at Constantinople on 4th October 1147. Eleanor and her husband were lavishly (albeit somewhat reluctantly) entertained by the Byzantine Emperor, Manuel I Comnenus; but they departed after twelve days, crossing the Bosporus and arriving in Nicea by the end of the month.

The army then marched further into Asia Minor taking the coastal route through Smyrna to Ephesus (where they spent Christmas) and then along the Meander valley and through the Phrygian mountains, with the objective of reaching the port of Attalia and from there taking ships to Saint Symeon near Antioch. The road to Attalia wound over the high desolate mountains of Paphlagonia and the conditions in January 1148 were appalling with storm force winds lashing down rain, snow and sleet, compounded by nightly numbing temperatures. By now Eleanor and her ladies in waiting were travelling in horse-drawn litters for protection against both the weather and the enemy, for the army was constantly harassed by bands of roving Turks. Finally the French were ambushed and routed on Mount Cadmos losing an estimated 7000 men, and the king barely escaped with his life. The survivors hurried on to Attalia only to discover there were too few available ships. Louis and his wife, together with many of the cavalry, sailed for Saint Symeon but their agony was not over as, due to atrocious weather, a normal three – day journey took three weeks. The remainder of the cavalry sailed over later but the foot-soldiers were abandoned and over half died while endeavouring to reach Antioch by the land route.

In late July 1148, and after brief periods in Antioch and Jerusalem, the Crusading armies invested Damascus, but following five days of struggle and with the imminence of further reinforcements for the Turks, the Christian leaders admitted defeat and the Second Crusade reached its ignominious conclusion. The whole adventure had been a disastrous failure. Eleanor having travelled many hundreds of miles, often in unimaginable discomfort and hazardous squalor, must have experienced a descent to Hades and (unlike Eurydice) a fortuitous release, during which she had shown courage, determination and resilience.

Her resolution was manifested again in 1152. Eleanor and Henry had met in Paris in the late summer of 1151 where there appears to have been an instant magnetism between them; and both were used to getting their own way. Immediately after the annulment of her first marriage in March 1152 she hurried to her Poitiers seat and sent envoys to Henry to come and marry her at once. This he did after clearing urgent matters of state, and they were married in Poitiers cathedral on the 18th May.

Her qualities were tested further when in 1168 she and Henry separated, the queen being exasperated by her husband's philandering. She returned to her French possessions and until 1173 presided over a glittering court in Poitiers which became the cultural capital of twelfth century Europe and, where it is claimed by some historians, chivalry was worshipped and troubadours composed and sang of courtly love. However, in the spring of 1173, while the queen was supporting her sons' rebellion against their father, she was apprehended and seized by the king's men and placed in custody by her husband, a confinement which she endured until Henry's death in 1189.

In September 1189 Richard was crowned king but then left the country in December to prepare for the Third Crusade, having appointed his mother regent in his absence. Returning from the crusade three years later Richard was detained near Vienna and handed over to the Emperor Henry VI who demanded an enormous ransom of 100,000 silver marks for his release. [25] Eleanor coordinated the raising of the ransom money and in December 1193, aged seventy, she sailed with her retinue across the North Sea and down the Rhine to Speyer where on 4th February 1194 Richard was released to her in exchange for the ransom money.

As the years passed her resilience seemed not to weaken since in 1199 with winter at its most bitter, and by now aged seventy seven, she journeyed south from Poitiers over the Pyrenees to Navarre and then Castile which she reached in January 1200. Her mission was to select one of the daughters of Eleanor of Castile (being her own granddaughter) to marry the heir to the French throne.

Equally remarkable, in 1202 when an octogenarian, she defended Mirebeau castle a few miles north-east of Poitiers in support of her son, John, against her grandson, Arthur of Brittany. She had become a nun at Fontevraud in Anjou in 1201 and on her death was buried in its abbey church.

3

THE YOUNG BECKET

At a distance of some eight centuries inevitably images are blurred, events uncertain and judgements must be tentative. However certain facts seem clear and established. Thomas Becket[26] was born in London's Cheapside on 21st December 1118, the son of Norman parents who had settled in England; his father, Gilbert Beket, (or Becket) being a middle class merchant from Rouen while his mother, Matilda, was a native of Caen. Gilbert was successful in business and was subsequently elected one of London's sheriffs. The Beckets had three daughters but only one son, who appears to have been very close to his mother. He was educated at Merton priory in Surrey followed by a London grammar school, possibly the one at St Paul's cathedral.

In his early teens Becket became very friendly with Richer de L'Aigle a Norman aristocrat who was at least twenty years older than Becket and whom the young Thomas had met when de L'Aigle lodged at the Becket family house while on business trips to London. De L'Aigle's father had been a courtier and he himself had a castle and estate at Pevensey in Sussex where Becket stayed for all of one summer, and where they went hawking and hunting together: pursuits which Becket loved and would prove useful to his career when years later he joined the royal court circle.

One can well understand an impressionable adolescent being highly flattered by the attention he received from a sophisticated, urbane, somewhat louche figure many years his senior. It appears that their relationship was intense and Becket's biographer John Guy and other historians have speculated as to its nature. The friendship may well have been unhealthy and sufficiently all consuming to persuade Becket's mother, when he was eighteen, to pack him off to Paris to study the humanities, including Latin, where his tutor was probably an Englishman, Robert of Melun.

Whilst not an outstanding academic Becket displayed more than competent administrative skills and showed himself to be a natural communicator and excellent negotiator. At the same time he appears to have led a punishing social life and quickly acquired the reputation of a dandy and man about town.

He spent about two years studying in Paris, returning to England only upon receiving news of his mother's death. However he did not go back to Paris possibly because his father was by now financially less secure following a number of fires which damaged or destroyed properties in which he had invested his savings – a constant hazard in medieval England.

The twelve months following Becket's return appear to have been a period of inconsequence, at the end of which he joined, as a clerk, the London banking business of a rich relation, Osbert Huitdeniers; he was fortunate in that his relatives were well connected, socially and commercially. During the years with Huitdeniers Becket's Parisian accomplishments were honed and expanded for he was clearly a thrusting, ambitious young man well aware of his own gifts, which included great energy, diligence, the ability to master a complex brief and perseverance in devoting as much of his time to it until all details were satisfactorily covered and digested. These qualities so impressed his friends that in 1145 they recommended the twenty six year old Becket to the Archbishop of Canterbury, Theobald, who engaged him as a notary in his household of exceptional young men. These included the future archbishop of York, Roger of Pont L'Eveque and two years later (in 1147) John of Salisbury [27] who became a lifelong friend of Becket. In this glittering galaxy his outstanding talents marked him out as "a brilliant member of a brilliant group". [28]

He joined a household which, like the monarch's, was always

on the move, covering as it did many parts of south east England as well as Canterbury; and it is likely that for the first part of his clerkship Becket practised the basic skills of office administration and helped with relatively humdrum matters such as arranging the transportation of an itinerant establishment.

In 1145, the same year in which Becket joined the archbishop, Bernard of Pisa was elected pope as Eugenius III. The new pope developed the doctrine of appeals to Rome from decisions based on canon law and reached by church courts throughout Europe relating to, inter alia, church property, contract, marriage, oaths and succession (i.e. rights of inheritance). Knowledge of, and expertise in, this legal corpus became essential, and the archbishop sent Becket to Bologna and Auxerre to study Roman and Canon law.

Theobald himself was not an outstanding academic but had considerable common sense and tact and, by the standards of his time, was fair and sensible in dealing with issues and other people. He was however no negotiator and nor did he possess powers of communication, both qualities which he soon recognised in Becket. The archbishop therefore came to rely on his pupil more and more to undertake on his behalf tasks of theological and political delicacy. The success of these was to be pivotal in Becket's career.

Of particular importance were two missions which Becket made to Rome at the archbishop's request. On the first occasion in 1149/50 he persuaded the pope to appoint Theobald as papal legate in England, thereby conferring on the archbishop the pope's authority and representative power over English theological and political disputes and events. On the second mission, undertaken shortly afterwards, Becket obtained a papal decree preventing the coronation of King Stephen's son, Eustace, as his father's successor and so potentially changing the course of British history. [29]

The outstanding success of these two briefs cemented Becket's position as being indispensable to the archbishop and triggered his move into public life. Pending this (albeit Becket was not yet a priest), a grateful archbishop secured his pupil's appointment to various sinecures within the church which provided a healthy income and financial independence for the ambitious clerk with expensive aspirations. His ascent of the ecclesiastical staircase was rapid as he acquired prebends at Lincoln and St Paul's cathedrals, the provost ship of Beverley and finally, in 1154, (almost certainly through the Archbishop's influence) the archdeaconry of Canterbury. Such breathless progress, however, was as nothing compared with what was to follow.

These personal incidents in Becket's life occurred during a period of great turbulence in British history, a time so severe as to be described 'the Anarchy' by historians. King Stephen reigned from 1135 to 1154, but of those nineteen years fifteen were subject to a savage civil war.

Its seeds were sown in 1127 when Henry I (the Conqueror's son) had pressured the baronage, including Stephen, into swearing under oath that they would accept the king's daughter, Matilda, and his only surviving legitimate child, as heiress to both the throne of England and the Duchy of Normandy. But on Henry's death in 1135 Stephen, judging his own claim to be legitimate, as William I's grandson through his mother Adela, and sacrificing honour for ambition, hastened from France to London where, with the support of its citizens, he seized the throne.

In order to provide a cloak of legitimacy for breaking his oath, it was claimed, falsely, that Henry I had disinherited Matilda just before he died. This villainy persuaded the barons to break their oaths as well, but unsurprisingly Matilda and her supporters resisted the whole charade and civil war ensued in May 1138. There followed one and a half decades of barbarism and savagery with the seizure and destruction of crops, numerous and unspeakable acts of torture, foreign mercenaries rampaging over the countryside and countless numbers of citizens dying from starvation, hypothermia and disease. The suffering, particularly in the southern areas of the country, was without precedent and a condemnation of man's inhumanity. It is to the historian a fascinating if chilling example of the human condition that the tribal nature of civil wars seems to unleash cruelty, devastation and wickedness of dimensions surpassing even those in conflicts between national states. The centuries following the Anarchy have given witness to such internal horrors in so many countries among which, after a lapse of nearly nine hundred years, France, Russia, Spain, Central Africa, Iraq and Syria stand out for their ferocity.

By 1153 the warring parties were exhausted and, with little prospect of either side emerging victorious, and the baronage unwilling to continue the conflict, fearful as they were of losing their estates in either England or France (or both), it was generally recognised that the time had come to attempt diplomacy. This process was initiated at Wallingford by Theobald who, as archbishop and papal legate, coupled with an emollient personality, had by now the greatest moral authority of any Englishman in public life. His position was strengthened by the fact that in 1147 he and pope Euginius had discreetly agreed to act in concert when confronted with problems affecting English political and public life;[30] and this secret accord might well have prevented Stephen from winning the civil war since, under it, the archbishop used his influence with the pope to persuade him to support the rebel cause.

The route to peace was assisted by the sudden death of Eustace in August 1153 and after some months of intense negotiations the archbishop, invariably accompanied and advised by Becket, effected a settlement which was ratified at the Council of Wallingford.[31] The agreed terms were that Matilda's son, Henry, (by now the undisputed leader of the opposition to Stephen) recognised Stephen as king of England for the rest of his life but with Stephen's surviving son, William, excluded from the succession; while Stephen, under oath, accepted Henry as his adopted son and heir to the throne.

This was a stunning achievement by Theobald and he was only too aware how much he owed to Becket for his constant diligence, support and advice in effecting the settlement. Twelve month later Stephen was dead and Henry was monarch. Both archbishop and his pupil might have been forgiven for thinking that Henry would be ever aware of his debt to them and perhaps conduct himself accordingly. Alas the psychology of debtors, which usually commences with gratitude, often changes to indifference, succeeded by the resentment of dependency.

4

THE CHANCELLOR

A few months later Theobald recommended Becket to Henry II (himself crowned king in December 1154) for the newly vacant office of chancellor. Henry agreed, and thus a future[32] clergyman became the nation's pre-eminent administrator on the 1st January 1155 and took the first step along the path which led to a tragedy of Aeschylean dimensions. Of course we know now with the benefit of judgments from both contemporary and subsequent scholars, from following the train of European events through succeeding centuries, from observing the behaviour of great men throughout history, that both Becket and Henry seemed to be, to use Hardy's analogy, mere playthings of the President of the Immortals in the tumult which engulfed them.

Indeed, future difficulties might well have been envisaged by all parties in that, despite the Concordat of Worms in 1122, and because of his supreme authority within his own extensive territories, and a quixotic temperament, Henry as previously suggested, was not inclined to submit to the papal reform movement. It is with this backcloth that Becket entered the king's service.

The office of chancellor was so all-embracing as to require its successful holder to have the diverse talents of a polymath, and in that sense the king must have felt he had acquired the ideal man.

Becket's duties as head of the royal writing office included guardianship of the royal seal and creating and enforcing government policy. He was also responsible for the administration of justice in the royal courts and collecting the royal revenues. Becket was particularly adept at obtaining money from landowners, which was the government's traditional source of income.

Furthermore, the chancellor in his new role stamped his personality on his public and social life: he lived lavishly with a household of about one hundred and fifty knights and their servants whose expenses were met out of state revenue. This extravagance extended to the sumptuous parties he held to entertain the king and baronage and foreign diplomats; parties on such a scale as to make even the late Lady Cunard and the Marchioness of Londonderry blanche with embarrassment. When criticised for these excesses he would defend his behaviour by pointing to his political and diplomatic successes benefitting both the monarch and nation.

Becket's coup de theatre came in 1158 when Henry sent him to Paris to negotiate with Louis Vii for the betrothal of Louis's new born daughter Margaret to Henry's three year old son Henry 'the Young King.' Becket travelled through France with over two hundred retainers on horseback, the party attired in exquisite apparel and enjoying unsurpassed luxury and accoutrements. The French king was charmed, agreed to the engagement and promised the restoration of the Vexin [33] to Henry on the marriage being effected.

If this represented the high tide of Becket's diplomacy then the following year, 1159, saw him as a man of action. Henry II, urged by his wife Eleanor, to recover her ancestral city and district of Toulouse which had been seized by Raymond V, assembled a force of knights and mercenaries to which an enthusiastic and bellicose Becket contributed 700 knights from his household and which he personally led into battle with panache and courage, albeit somewhat fortuitously, in view of the foolhardy risks he apparently took during forays into the Vexin and Quercy. Although Toulouse was not recovered due to its massive fortifications Louis VII agreed to Henry retaining the Vexin and land and buildings captured in Quercy.

This campaign also threw into relief the personal relationship between the monarch and his chancellor. The received position among most historians was that Henry and Becket enjoyed a friendship which appeared to have been close, warm and with great admiration for each other's ability and qualities. Indeed it was claimed that the king regarded Becket as his closest friend; so much so that Henry sent his eldest son, Henry 'the Young King', to live with Becket for a time. In support of this position is the fact that Becket's contemporary, friend and biographer, William fitz Stephen wrote "Never in the whole epoch of Christian history were two men more of one mind or better friends".

Furthermore Henry and Becket spent many days and nights together hunting, feasting and generally roistering – although it seems that, unlike the king, Becket remained celibate.

All of this appears to point to a strong mutual friendship; however some historians (notably John Guy) have cast doubt on the strength of the friendship and point to a major disagreement between the king and chancellor during a council of war to decide whether to invest the city of Toulouse. The king and baronage were for abandoning the proposed siege – as the city seemed to be impregnable – and instead proposed to attack softer targets nearby. Becket insisted on proceeding with the siege until overruled by the monarch who displayed considerable Angevin anger with Becket's intransigence.

The truth may well be that, because he was a despotic figure, Henry wanted a friendship with Becket while it was on his own terms and both suited his convenience and advanced his policies; but it was always to be a relationship of master and servant.

5

THE ARCHBISHOP

For some seven years the chancellor was the chief architect of national policy, an important ingredient of which was asserting the crown's primacy over the church, and thus resistance to, not to say rejection of, interference or direction from Rome. Then in 1162 Theobald died leaving a vacancy for the See of Canterbury. One can but imagine the king's feelings on receiving the news from Kent. He must have reasoned that this was a gilt edged opportunity to insert his trusted friend into the very kernel of ecclesiastical power and so ensure the monarch's interests would be enhanced at the expense of the Vatican. Accordingly, Henry bullied the clergy into accepting Becket as archbishop of Canterbury.

The reaction of Becket himself however was entirely different. More prescient than his master, the chancellor foresaw the impossibility of reconciling the role of supreme English prelate with that of the nation's chief executive. He therefore vehemently resisted the proposed appointment. Is it perhaps fanciful to conject that Becket had a portent of the disaster to come? Certain it is however that he realised acceptance of the archbishopric would mean primary loyalty and indeed fealty to God and to Rome, at the expense of duty to his monarch, and that compromise would be unthinkable.

However the king remained adamant and eventually Becket acceded to his master's wishes and was consecrated archbishop by the bishop of Winchester on 3rd June 1162. Here there is a double irony: Theobald had urged the appointment of Becket as chancellor primarily so that the church would have a friend at the heart of government to protect the church's interests. The king appointed Becket to achieve the opposite: both men were to be disappointed. Perhaps the supreme irony is that Becket, the man who as chancellor rejected papal interference in English church affairs, was now appointed to the most important position in that institution.

Becket's election as archbishop had been ratified at the Westminster council held on the 23rd May 1162 with only one dissenting voice: that of Gilbert Foliot, bishop of Hereford. Foliot had no time for Becket whom he regarded as an upstart, a view which was no doubt fuelled by the god of envy. How ironic it is therefore that more than eight hundred and fifty years later Herefordshire still remains one of the English Counties containing at least two churches dedicated to his memory.

Perhaps the most interesting result of all this was the psychological change in the new archbishop in that overnight it seems the man of action became a contemplative, the epicurean a stoic, the lover of extravagance an apostle of asceticism, the hunter and dandy a votary, the defier of Rome, its greatest defender. All seemed to point to a life of piety and tranquillity.

Yet storm clouds gathered in the autumn of 1162 when Becket resigned the chancellorship pleading an inability to carry out his governmental duties because of his church commitments. His fatal mistake was that he resigned before consulting the monarch. This conduct provoked a mighty Angevin rage and it should be remembered that the scene was now set for a titanic struggle between two of the most powerful, impressive and intractable figures of their age. Seldom in British history have there been men of such stature each determined to bend the other to his will in the management of their church and country.

Henry, one of our greatest monarchs, ruled his English and substantial French possessions with despotic power. As referred to earlier, a highly competent administrator and outstanding military figure, he was well aware of his own abilities and this, combined with a renowned temper, made him a dangerous opponent. Furthermore, he was married to the most imposing and fascinating woman of the late Middle Ages. Early in their marriage they must have seemed a couple capable of dominating the Continent let alone one man, unless Becket could now so charm the queen as to make her his ally.

In his turn Becket was fastidious, hard working, obstinate and tactless, fully convinced that he was right and a man to whom compromise was unknown.

Such disparate and forthright personalities created an incendiary situation and, following some early but minor disagreements after the archbishop's enthronement,[34] a major eruption occurred at the council of Westminster in the October of 1163 with the king's proposal that clergy convicted of crimes by the ecclesiastical courts should nevertheless be punished by the royal courts. Becket rejected this on the Hildebrandian grounds that clergy were subject only to the laws of God. The bishops, many of whom had originally sympathised with Henry's position, were won over by Becket's contention and therefore rejected the king's demands. Henry, to mark his displeasure, immediately removed his son Henry the Young King from Becket's household and terminated his guardianship.

Later in the month the king and archbishop met near Northampton to try to reach an agreement and effect a reconciliation but both men failed to compromise and, indeed, apparently used strong language and parted on worse terms than before their meeting.

The impasse which ensued seemed intractable but Becket appealed to Pope Alexander III, then living at Sens in France as an exile from Rome. Alexander was in some difficulty because Henry had supported him against the claims of the antipope Paschal III[35] and, moreover, the pope feared driving Henry into the arms of Barbarossa. He therefore responded by letter and legate urging Becket to compromise, while reinforcing this advice by despatching to England as his envoy Abbot Philip of Aumone, who assured the archbishop that Henry would merely require an oral concession. Becket felt isolated, particularly as his closest friend, John of Salisbury, was himself living in exile, and unable to give him much needed support.

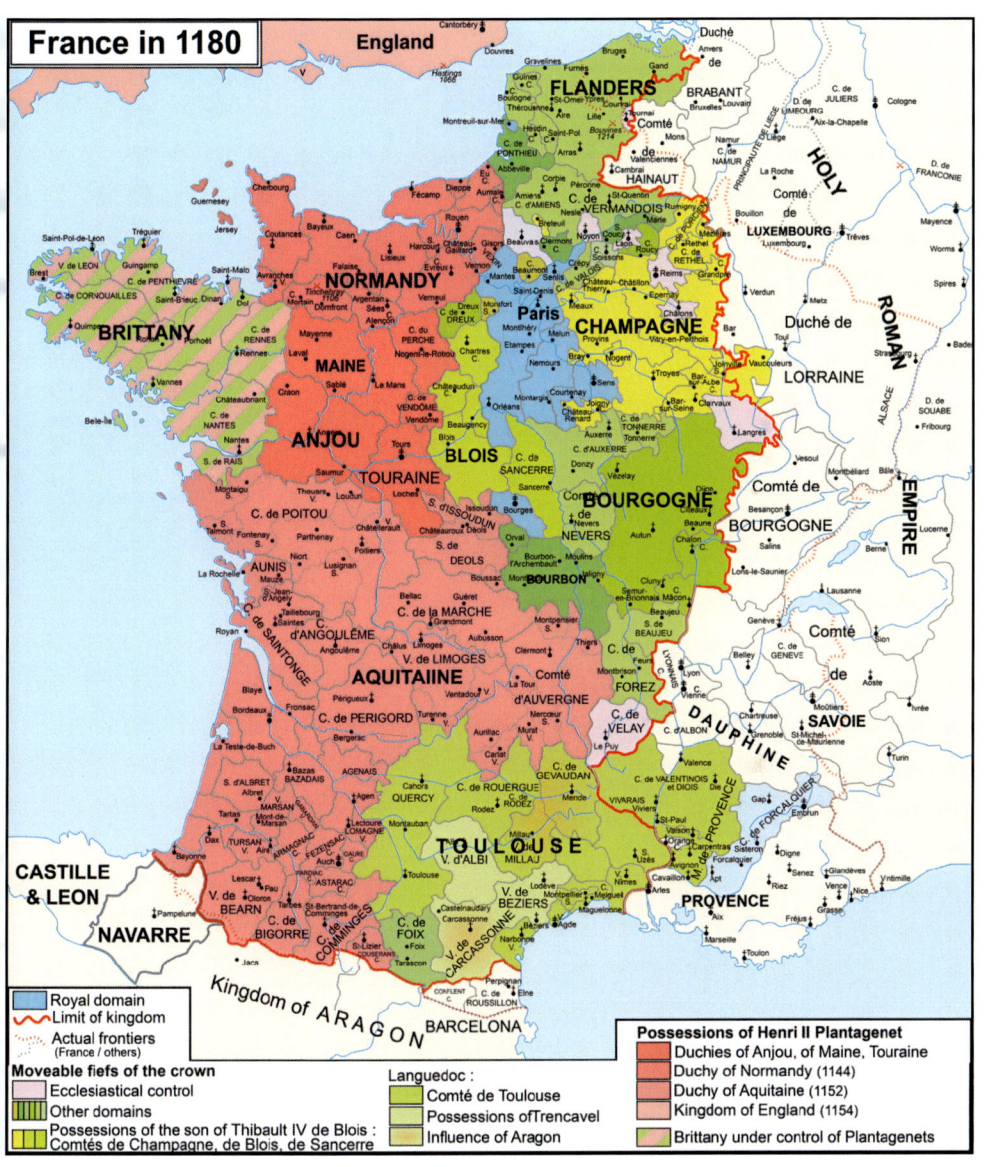

France in 1180

The Pope – Alexander III

The King of France –
Louis VII

The Holy Roman Emperor –
Frederick I 'Barbarossa'

The Holy Roman Empire around 1080

The Crusades – the route of the Second Crusade (in blue) starting at Ratisbon

Raymond of Poitiers welcoming Louis VII in Antioch

Henry II – King of England

Effigy of Eleanor of Aquitaine

Fontevraud Abbey in the Loire Valley contains the tombs of
Eleanor of Aquitaine, Henry II and their son, Richard I

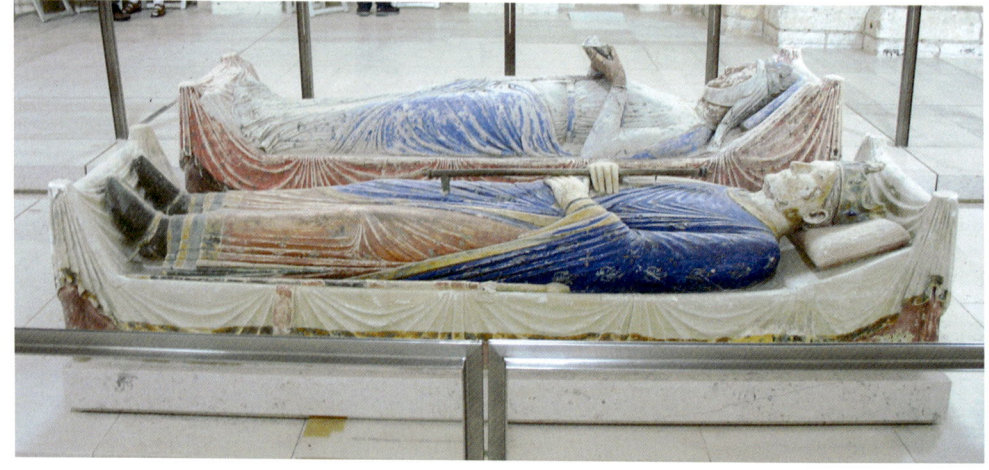

The tombs of Eleanor of Aquitaine and Henry II in Fontevraud Abbey

Thomas Becket –
detail from a window at Canterbury Cathedral

Thomas Becket –
a carving at Sens Cathedral

Above left: A late 15th century alabaster panel representing the martyrdom of Thomas Becket

Above right: A cast lead pilgrim badge of St Thomas Becket, sold in great numbers to those who made the pilgrimage to Canterbury Cathedral

Left: The Murder of Thomas A Becket, as depicted in *Pictures of English History* (1888)

The Thomas Becket Altar in Canterbury Cathedral –
the dramatic sculpture is the work of Giles Blomfield of Truro

Thus in December 1163 at Oxford the archbishop, by now worn down from pressures applied to him by the king, court and curia, precipitously withdrew his objections and, much to the anger of the bishops, Henry prevailed. The king, exalting in his victory, now planned revenge.

Henry retaliated in January 1164 by convening the Clarendon Council, in his Wiltshire hunting-lodge of that name, in which he insisted the role of the English church should be returned to that which it had held during the reign of the king's grandfather, Henry I. The church's position was to be enshrined in the sixteen 'Constitutions' of Clarendon, which purported to codify the 'customs' as they existed and were practised in Henry I's reign and provided, *inter alia*, that in addition to clergy being subject to the royal courts, the royal consent would be required before an appeal to Rome, the excommunication [36] of any baron, or for any bishop wishing to leave the country. In addition the monarch was to be the arbitrator of episcopal elections.

This is where the monarch overcalled his hand when, instead of accepting Becket's capitulation at Oxford and, in breach of his own assurance to the papal legate that an oral concession would suffice, he now demanded written codification and a public humiliation for the archbishop.

However, during the twenty years since the death of Henry I the English church had gradually acquired greater autonomy and had extended its authority over more and more facets of religious and secular life. Having tasted the heady wine of increased freedom and prestige the church's leaders were not now to be deprived of what had become familiar and indeed normal. Therefore, led by their archbishop, the bishops rejected the Constitutions.

But no sooner had Becket overseen this resistance than, to the amazement of his colleagues, he changed his mind and agreed to the proposed Constitutions. This volte-face at a stroke completed the alienation of both the king and his own clergy; Henry, intoxicated by his success, now considered his riposte. As for the archbishop, it may be that weeks of pressure from so many sources had led to a personal crisis of confidence and affected his ability to make sustainable decisions. This is suggested by the fact that almost immediately after Becket agreed to the Constitutions he expressed regret and remorse for having yielded and then repudiated his earlier submission.

He had therefore varied his position on this fundamental issue on five occasions; vacillation which was not conduct suggesting firm leadership. Perhaps the archbishop's only consolation was that at last pope Alexander gave him substantial support in rejecting the codification of the 'customs' – no doubt emboldened by the recent death of the anti-pope Victor IV and therefore less fearful of alienating Henry II.

Meanwhile the king, not satisfied with the denouement at Clarendon, was determined to punish Becket severely. The animosity between monarch and archbishop had extended from disagreement over important political and philosophical beliefs to profound personal aversion, at least on the part of Henry, who now displayed all the unpleasant behaviour of a self-confident despot. Both the pope and Becket's friend John of Salisbury, fearful of the king's dangerous mood, advised the archbishop to exercise extreme caution when dealing with him.

Henry's retribution began when the primate was ordered to attend the king's court but failed to appear, and so his vengeful monarch pursued him on charges of contempt of court and corruption as chancellor. The proceedings were held at the Council of Northampton in October 1164. This council was an assembly which, to the modern reader, would have been redolent of the Communist show trials held in Russia in the 1930s and in Eastern Europe after the Second World War. Their common pattern was that the verdict and punishment were decided beforehand and the sole purpose of the proceedings was to produce as much 'testimony' as possible from bribed and/or tortured witnesses, in an attempt to legitimate a travesty.

6

THE EXILE

Becket attended the Council but, seeing and hearing of the force and inducements applied to the bishops and barons by Henry, and realising the inevitable verdict, he speedily left. With the word "Traitor" hissing from every corner of the chamber and ringing in his ears he must have felt he had been abandoned to the Furies and so he fled to France from the priory near Northampton where he had been staying, disguised as a Cluniac lay brother and accompanied only by three loyal servants. The party travelled at night and by devious routes to avoid capture, and some days later sailed from Sandwich to France, beaching their boat near Gravelines a few miles south west of Dunkirk.

As the archbishop and his tiny party rode through the bleak countryside of northern France in late autumn, Becket may well have reflected on his previous journey some six years before, leading two hundred retainers so caparisoned as to dazzle the country people with their brilliance and luxurious display as they passed through the villages with flags fluttering, weaponry clanking, the weight of provisions filling the creaking supply wagons, and then finally overwhelming the French king in Paris with charm as Becket achieved his greatest diplomatic coup.

How different the current venture for a man whose public triumphs lay in the past, a man disguised in coarse habit with a mere handful of followers, hounded by Henry's allies, fearing capture by his enemies round every curve of the highway, creeping through towns and villages in constant danger of exposure, a man whose dreams had been rent and thwarted by a capricious bully; a figure now feeling mortality like the leaves of autumn, bronzed and brittle in a hostile wind.

The archbishop and his retinue travelled to Soissons, sixty or so miles north east of Paris, where Becket met Louis VII. It seems that the French king admired Becket for his undoubted talents and also liked him personally, being captivated by Becket's charm and manner. But while Louis promised the archbishop as much help as possible he made it clear that he was not prepared to upset Henry and compromise the treaty between the two countries which had been initiated by Becket himself in 1158.

The archbishop's next objective was to enlist further support from Pope Alexander III who was also living in exile, at Sens in northern Burgundy. Accordingly, Becket rode south to Sens where the pope received him sympathetically, insisted he should retain his archbishopric, but ordered him to live in the Cistercian abbey at Pontigny near Auxerre with a few companions, and not to return to England until after any rapprochement with Henry. In fact Becket was to remain at Putigny for nearly two years leading a life of prayer and scholarship, while conducting a substantial and sustained correspondence with his friends and supporters.

As for the pope, his own position remained fragile. Alexander was the most nomadic of popes, spending between sixteen and seventeen years of his twenty-two years papacy in exile, either in France or elsewhere in Italy;[37] and during that period he had to endure four anti-popes elected at the behest of the Holy Roman Emperor, each claiming legitimacy and undermining the pontiff's authority and security. This became evident in May of the following year (1165) at the Council of Wurzburg when the German clergy swore under oath to Barbarossa not to recognise Alexander as pope but rather to accept the recently elected anti-pope Paschal III as the legitimate pontiff. Alexander was concerned that this could prove to be contagious and it is therefore understandable that his support for Becket was largely covert.

While the archbishop was adjusting to a new life in exile Henry exacted a savage revenge in England: Becket's property was seized, his relations, retainers, supporters and their families were deported to France, and money due to the papacy was withheld. The pope badly needed more income which was another reason for him to be discreet in his dealings with the archbishop. However in November 1165 Alexander was able to return to Rome and to a rapturous reception from its citizens. This stiffened his resolve and, on discovering that Henry now wished to reach an accommodation with Barbarossa, – the pope's foremost antagonist – Alexander responded forcefully by actively inciting Becket to harden his position in dealing with Henry and then, in May 1166, by appointing the archbishop his papal legate to England.

Fortified by his new powers, and now with the pope's full confidence, in June 1166 the archbishop delivered a fiery sermon in the abbey of Vezelay, in which he robustly defended his position and then excommunicated a number of clergy and public figures who had sided with the king over the Constitutions of Clarendon, or had subsequently plundered church property or harried the archbishop's supporters. But one major error by Becket was to include on his list Jocelin de Bailleul, for de Bailleul was the head of Queen Eleanor's household and she was furious at the excommunication.

Furthermore, while the archbishop did not excommunicate the king himself, the threat of such action was implicit; this outraged Henry who demanded Becket's dismissal by the pope, failing which he threatened to recognise the anti-pope. Alexander resisted this but, by October 1166, Barbarossa's army was descending on northern Italy and, with every soldier's step south, the pope's resolve weakened; therefore he suspended Becket's powers of excommunication while refusing to dismiss or suspend the archbishop himself. Then in November of that year Becket and his companions were ejected from Pontigny through pressure applied by Henry. They withdrew to Sens where Louis VII granted them shelter and guaranteed their safety in the abbey.

In June 1167 the German army entered Rome and the pope fled to Benevento while the anti-pope Guy of Crema was installed as

Paschal III. However, much to the relief of Alexander, by August the invading army was consumed by malaria, thousands died, and the demoralized remnants abandoned Rome, retreating north back to Germany and harried along the way over the plains of Lombardy and through the Alpine passes, by members of the Lombard League.

Meanwhile, Louis VII, in contrast to the pope, now became more robust. For some years the English and French had sparred fitfully in Brittany, the Vexin and Poitou and the French monarch, by now appalled by Henry's bullying, and perhaps sensing an opportunity to expand his country's frontiers, initiated military action against the English in the Vexin and elsewhere. However, while this distracted Henry for some months, other political events menaced the positions of both the French king and pope Alexander, for in 1168 Henry 'the Lion' Duke of Saxony and Bavaria – and Barbarossa's cousin – married Henry II's daughter Matilda. This strengthened the ties between Frederick and the English king and threatened the balance of power in Europe, since although the emperor was somewhat enervated by his continuing struggle with the Lombard League, his influence remained considerable, so that on the 9th September 1166 Abbot John of Struma was elected anti-pope as Calixtus III in succession to Paschal III; a procedure carried out under the auspices of Frederick.

These international developments had a profound impact upon Becket's personal and public life during the six years of exile and despite, or perhaps because of, the oscillations of political and military power in Europe the parties to the estrangement and their supporters and advisors made numerous attempts at reconciliation. There were two abortive efforts to arrange a meeting in the spring of 1165. Then the following year two papal mediators, William of Pavia and Otto of Brescia, were appointed by Alexander at Henry's request, but proved to be ineffective. They met the archbishop near Gisors in November 1167 but failed to persuade him to agree to the 'customs' informally and without any documentation: Becket clearly saw this suggestion as blatant hypocrisy.

However, early in 1168 the pope appointed two new mediators, Simon of Mont-Dieu and Bernard de la Coudre. These proved to be more satisfactory than their predecessors in that they approached the disputed matters without predetermined positions or prejudices. War weariness and the aforesaid appointments led to a meeting of Louis and Henry at Montmirail south west of Chartres in January 1169 to settle the military disputes between the two monarchs and make peace on terms that provided for Henry's son Henry 'the Young King', by now married to Louis's daughter Margaret, to inherit England, Normandy, Anjou and Maine. Following this, Becket was summoned to appear and reach a modus operandi with Henry. This he agreed with the new papal arbitrators, but when appearing before the two monarchs he again – and much to Henry's outrage – exempted himself from observing the 'customs' where they conflicted with his duty to God.

This seemed to leave the archbishop isolated until shortly afterwards Louis, by now tired of Henry's duplicitous behaviour, boorishness and military excesses, promised Becket his full support and protection in dealing with the English king. Over the centuries historians have not in general been kind to Louis VII, portraying him as a weak, if not feeble, figure incapable of resolution and unable to make decisions. However, in his dealing with Becket this does not appear to be so, in that the king showed himself to be a loyal friend and the most reliable ally of the archbishop among the leading European figures of his time. No doubt his support for Becket was influenced also by national interest and his wish to extend France's frontiers and restore her power and influence at the expense of England; but despite this, to the archbishop he was steadfast.

The collapse of peace talks at Montmirail was followed by another failure in February, at St-Leger-en-Yvelines near Rambouillet in the Vexin. These new negotiations, led by the pope's mediators, failed primarily because Henry still insisted upon Becket and his supporters agreeing to observe the 'customs'. The arbitrators were exasperated and thereupon served notice on the king to restore forthwith, to the archbishop and his followers, all their sequestered property, failing which further action would be taken by the Vatican.

In order to reinforce the pressure now being exerted on Henry,

Becket travelled to Clairvaux abbey in north-east France at Easter where he excommunicated more of the king's sympathisers. This action was again suspended at the pope's wish until his new mediators, Vivian of Orvieto and Gratian of Pisa, had met Henry. In fact meetings took place on four occasions in the late summer of 1169 at a time when Henry was chasing rebels in Aquitaine. Whether the king was intoxicated by the excitement of war and pursuit of power is speculative, but what is certain is that his behaviour at these meetings was erratic at the least, and the bully always prevailed over the conciliator.

Finally, exasperated by the failure to reach an accord on the perennial problem of the 'customs' and outraged by Becket's new decision to impose the suspended excommunications proclaimed at Clairvaux, Henry announced savagely punitive measures for his English subjects, worthy of a modern police state: those complying with an interdict were to be deported along with their families, appeals to the pope or archbishop were prohibited, clergymen were not to leave the country without a permit, the remaining property of Becket's supporters was to be seized, and all males over the age of fifteen were to swear an oath of compliance.

Despite the failures of the peace conferences at Montmirail and St-Leger, in November 1169 yet another attempt was made, this time at Montmartre just north of Paris. The negotiations produced agreement, including provisions for Henry to return the seized property, and recognition of the Church's special status releasing it from certain of the 'customs'. At last all seemed to be resolved, however it appeared that the punitive gods were unable to resist a final act of interference. The practice was for peace terms to be sealed by the kiss of peace, but Henry refused to kiss the archbishop, and then dissembled in claiming that he was bound by a prior oath to the contrary. This last minute obstacle, which terminated the conference, was both a major blow to the exiles and particularly surprising, since by now the French and English monarchs had a common interest in securing peace terms, as each was anxious to implement the coronation of Henry 'the Young King' and Margaret and so secure the English succession.

Great expectations dissolved in a cocktail of vanity and intransigence.

Becket's reaction to the failure was to activate the Clairvaux excommunications with additions, and to threaten a general interdict[38] on England, coupled with the excommunication of its monarch, unless Henry agreed to observe the proposed peace terms; but yet again the pope, at Henry's behest, agreed to delay the imposition of the interdict.

Meanwhile Henry was determined to proceed with the coronation of his son, and on the 14th June 1170 'the Young King' was crowned by Roger of Pont L'Eveque, the archbishop of York, assisted by Gilbert Foliot, now bishop of London, and Jocelin bishop of Salisbury. This ceremony was performed in defiance of both the pope and Becket himself whose right it was, as archbishop of Canterbury, to conduct the coronation. The act of disobedience by the three bishops was compounded by not including Margaret in the proceedings, an extraordinary oversight which deeply upset the French king.[39]

At the same time the pope's patience with Henry was at last exhausted and he insisted that the king attend a peace conference to agree terms similar to those finalised at Montmartre. Pending this, Alexander instructed his legates and Becket to place a general interdict on all of Henry's territories. This papal action was sufficient to propel Henry towards such a conference, which was held in July at Freteval, about one hundred miles south of Paris in central France. In a spirit of reconciliation Becket agreed not to demand the kiss of peace.

The primate, prematurely aged by the travails of exile, and Henry, concerned to avoid the interdicts, had a mutual interest in a speedy settlement. So it was that after six years of hopes unfulfilled, scores of friendships strained and thousands of civil servants' hours squandered, an agreement was reached in the afternoon of the third day; on terms not dissimilar to those accepted at the abortive Montmartre meeting.

However, the prickly temperament of the one party and the wounded pride of the other, did not suggest confidence in a permanent peace between them. It was a victory for common sense tarnished by future uncertainty as demonstrated by the fact that in the following few months Becket, while exercising self discipline, could not at the same time resist opportunities to quibble over the minutiae of the peace agreement; while the king appeared to manipulate it on every possible occasion and certainly failed to observe its spirit.

7

THE MURDER

It had been agreed that the primate would return to England in November 1170 but in fact he sailed on the first of December and landed at Sandwich. Ominously, it appeared that many of the exiles' properties seized by Henry's supporters had not been returned to their legal owners, in breach of the Freteval accord. Furthermore other estates had been plundered and despoiled by the king's more infamous stooges – notoriously Ranulf de Broc and his nephew Robert. However, despite this unpromising state of affairs, Becket travelled from the coast to Canterbury on horseback and must have been encouraged by his reception: cheering crowds lined his route and it seems bells of welcome rang out in all the villages, while the celebrations in Canterbury were equally euphoric.

A few days after arriving in Canterbury the archbishop left for London, (where he was again well-received by enthusiastic citizens), in the hope of meeting and restoring cordial relations with his former pupil, Henry 'the Young King', whose court was at Woodstock.

Not only did Henry refuse to see Becket but informed him, through underlings, that he was to return to Canterbury immediately and not to venture into any other town. This must have been a bitter experience for the primate and emphasized the threat to him from at least a section of the secular establishment.

The archbishop had arrived in Canterbury armed with orders from Pope Alexander suspending and excommunicating the three 'coronation' bishops for, inter alia, crowning 'the Young King' in defiance of the Vatican. These bishops had already sent to 'the Young King' a false claim that Becket was proposing to dethrone him on the grounds that conduct of the coronation ceremony was the sole prerogative of the archbishop of Canterbury. They now hastened to Normandy and Henry's court where, having sent in advance copies of their excommunications, they shamelessly announced that Becket was doubting the validity of the coronation. The king's anger was volcanic and, accusing Becket of breaching the terms of the Freteval accord, he summoned a council which met at Bur-le-Roi in late December, where it tried and convicted the primate of treason in his absence and ordered that he be apprehended and incarcerated.

At or around the time of these proceedings Henry in his fury was alleged to have shouted words which may or may not have been, "who will rid me of this turbulent priest?" but which conveyed a similar meaning. The question may have been rhetorical but it was answered by action. Four young knights, Richard le Breton (also known as 'Brito') Hugh de Morville, William de Tracy and Reginald fitz Urse, no doubt anxious for early promotion in the hothouse which was the Angevin court circle, saddled their horses and cantered westwards; probably picturing great estates and grand titles to be showered upon them by a grateful monarch. They crossed the Channel and arrived in Canterbury on the 29th December 1170.

On Christmas day in the cathedral Becket had denounced and excommunicated from the pulpit those still illegally occupying church property – in breach of the Freteval settlement – and made particular reference to the de Brocs who were self seekers of the worst kind and characteristic of the human flotsam which somehow surfaces under despotic regimes. As Christmas recipients of Becket's verbal laceration they were only too pleased to co-operate with the four knights.

Therefore they and their ruffianly followers sealed off all exits from the city while fitz Urse and his co-conspirators went to the archbishop's palace and, leaving their weapons outside, they entered the great hall where they found dinner was ending, it being late afternoon. They called for Becket and, on his arrival, there was an angry conversation, with Reginald fitz Urse accusing the archbishop of breaking the peace terms and betraying the king; charges which Becket vigorously rejected. The four knights then stormed out after making it clear that they would shortly return.

It has been suggested that the archbishop should have been more diplomatic in answering fitz Urse, but he was dealing with hot headed irrational young bucks fired up by alcohol and prospects of glory, with blood on their minds and murder in their hearts. It is unlikely that whatever Becket said could have changed the course of events.

It was now dusk, and, soon after, the bells for vespers rang out, prompting the archbishop to walk from his palace into the cathedral. Although the monks begged him to have the cathedral doors locked and so exclude his enemies, he would not hear of this in "a house of prayer". He had reached the north transept and was standing by its east wall when the would be assassins and their followers, now fully armed, burst in from the cloisters. Men of violence mingled with the peaceful congregation, and equally mixed were the emotions of hatred, fear, outrage, courage and compassion competing for supremacy. That evening witnessed the triumph of wickedness. Following more angry words, and with de Morville restraining the crowd, fitz Urse urged on the other two knights to carry out their hideous crime. The primate was seized and de Tracy felled him with two blows from his sword. While he was barely conscious le Breton struck him with such ferocity as to remove the top part of his head and in the process shatter the assailant's sword.

This villainy was compounded when the knights and their followers immediately left the cathedral to join the de Brocs in ransacking the palace and stealing everything of value.

A sorrowful monk collected up as much of the dead man's blood and brains as he could, to preserve as sacred relics. So died a remarkable, if controversial, man. He was fifty years of age.

8

THE CONSEQUENCE

News of the appalling events in Canterbury cathedral created reverberations throughout the Christian world, where it was received with horror. As for Henry II, his position was unenviable. He certainly affected sorrow in an attempt to pacify the pope and protect his own reputation; but the pontiff's papal legate for France, William Sens, imposed a general interdict on all the king's territories in continental Europe. In addition Alexander barred Henry from all churches until he had received absolution from the pope's two papal legates, cardinals Albert de Morra and Theodwin of San Vitale.

This took place in May 1172 with the king on his knees outside Avranches cathedral in Normandy, and after Henry had sworn that he had neither demanded nor wished for Becket's death.

It may be argued that this oath contradicted the facts. However, it should be remembered that in many ways the master of the greatest realm in Europe was also as a petulant child who frets when denied his toys for a minor misdemeanour, and then shrieks for their restoration. Thus Henry, when thwarted, would frequently throw himself to the floor howling and kicking his legs in the air with fury. Minutes later the tantrum would cease, clouds pass over, and the sunshine of tranquillity return. So it may be that the four knights took literally what was in fact a mere display of Angevin transient temper; with fatal and disastrous consequences.

The king agreed also that appeals to the pope should be allowed without hindrance and that all confiscated property would be restored to the church and the exiles. In addition Henry pledged an amnesty to the exiles on their return and agreed to cancel all 'customs' initiated during his reign which adversely affected the church. Finally he swore allegiance to the pope under oath.

These were very substantial concessions by the state to the church and were fortified when, in 1176, the king promised that in future all criminous clergy should be tried and sentenced in the ecclesiastical courts. Thus it was that virtually all of Becket's aims came to fulfilment; but at a terrible cost. The monarch retained the right to participate in (and in reality decide upon) the appointment of bishops but most other ecclesiastical matters remained, or became, the sole prerogative of the church.

In July 1174, at a difficult time in his military campaigns, Henry went to Canterbury, walked bare footed from St Dunstan's chapel to the cathedral, and knelt in prayer before the martyr's tomb while confessing his role in the archbishop's death. He was lightly beaten with rods by clergy and remained there in prayer until the following morning when he attended a service. So it seems that the king's public political concessions may have been followed by an attempt to achieve a posthumous personal reconciliation with an old friend.

Henry outlived the archbishop by eighteen years and these were generally years of military glory – in Ireland, Scotland, Normandy and Brittany as well as suppressed risings and rebellions in England, Anjou, Poitou, and Aquitaine. But the public successes came to a saddened and lonely man whose four ambitious sons, encouraged and supported by their embittered mother, by now estranged from her husband and living in custody in England, plotted against their father on four occasions.

Therefore Henry spent much of his time between 1173 and 1189 fighting the Scots, the French and his own family. Can military honour and international acclaim ever compensate for filial betrayal?

Finally, in 1189, the king, by now very ill, was defeated at Le Mans. As he lay dying he was shown a list of his opponents and conspirators: it was headed by his youngest and favourite son, John.

Henry died murmuring: "Let things go as they will. Shame, shame on a conquered king".

The impact of the archbishop's murder upon Christians was enormous, and the middle class merchant's son whose rise through the echelons of both the state and the church had been so swift and so high, was now venerated as a martyr. The required miracles were apparently performed with the treasured blood and brains effecting numerous cures for disabilities and diseases. They were at least sufficient to satisfy the papal curia, and on the 21st February 1173 Thomas Becket was canonised by pope Alexander.

For more than eight hundred years men and women from all over the world have travelled as pilgrims and visitors to Canterbury by air, ship, rail, car, bicycle, on horseback and on foot. Every year more than one million people [40] arrive to worship at the spot where Thomas Becket was cut down. [41]

It may be wondered by the reader why the tiny church in the remote hamlet of Huntington in North West Herefordshire, a building which appears to have been constructed early in the twelfth century, was dedicated to St Thomas Becket?

It has been suggested that Richard le Breton founded the church as a penance. However, the author is unable to discover any connection between le Breton and the Welsh Marches, since his family estates were in Devon. The most likely explanation is that St Thomas was a very fashionable saint in the decades following his canonisation, and it would have been natural for whoever was responsible for the church, to dedicate it to St Thomas's memory. Later, the very remoteness of the building probably saved it from the attention of Henry VIII and his underlings.

Meanwhile, le Breton and the other three murderers, following their Canterbury abomination, fled north to de Morville's estate in north Yorkshire where it appears that they lived well for some months until Easter 1171, when pope Alexander excommunicated them and imposed the punishment of fourteen years exile in the Holy Land. It seems they arrived there in 1173. All four died there and apparently were buried outside the Temple in Jerusalem.

9

SUMMATION

The reader may well ask why this narrative contains so little mention of Queen Eleanor and her role, if any, in an extraordinary drama. The answer is partly that contemporary sources are largely silent and the historian must rely upon conjecture and possibility. Some historians (and most recently, John Guy) question whether Eleanor had much control over Henry, and indeed suggest that her independent influence was minimal.

The author has reservations about this since she had such a forceful personality and spirit. In addition she probably reminded Henry from time to time that she had brought to the marriage vast domains and subsequently provided him with an abundance of heirs.

It seems therefore that had she wished she could have influenced the king's behaviour in Becket's interest. The fact that she did not do so is evidenced in a letter written in 1165 to the primate by his old friend John of Salisbury, in which John warns Becket that he must not expect any help from the queen. Some years later the queen displayed her metier when supporting the revolts of her sons against their father. Had Becket, earlier in his career, used his diplomatic skills to recruit Eleanor to his cause, he would have acquired a powerful advocate, and the river of history may well have changed its course; that Becket appears not to have done so was a political blunder.

Queen Eleanor's biographer, Amy Kelly, suggests [42] that Becket's intimate social relationship with the king while he was chancellor, marginalised the queen who not unnaturally bitterly resented her perceived isolation.

However this is denied by Alison Weir in her biography, *Eleanor of Aquitaine*, in which she writes: "History does not record what Queen Eleanor thought of this friendship during these early years, although several historians have perceptively suggested that it relegated her to the side-lines of affairs and undermined her influence with the king. There is no evidence that the Queen slighted Becket or bore him any malice during the period of his chancellorship. It may even have humoured her to take an opposite stance to her mother-in-law, the Empress Matilda, who disapproved of Becket and made no bones about saying so".

The true position will probably remain uncertain. But a formidable woman who, at the age of seventy seven, was to cross the Pyrenees, in winter, in medieval Europe, and who possessed social and political connections throughout the continent, was unlikely to tolerate being excluded from public life nor remain silent when important matters of state were discussed and decided.

In any event, by the autumn of 1166 the royal marriage was at best semi-detached; Henry's many infidelities would have tried the tolerance of any wife let alone one so capricious as Eleanor. It seems likely that her influence over her husband diminished in proportion to their ardour. Furthermore, Becket in excommunicating Jocelin de Bailleul, the head of the Queen's household, did little to encourage Eleanor in furthering his cause.

Therefore it appears quite possible that the Queen's initial support for her husband crumbled along with her marriage, until the murder provoked her open hostility; by which time it was of course too late to save the archbishop.

If early hubris and insensitivity by Becket prevented a firm friendship with the queen, a friendship which could have secured his position after relinquishing the chancellorship, and provided a firm ally at court, the archbishop's relations with king Louis VII of France were never in doubt. As previously stated, the French king was highly impressed by Becket's ability and won over by his personality: he admired the gifts and was enchanted by the charm. The problem was, however, that the king's ability to influence events was strictly limited.

Aquitaine was eight times the size of the small royal kingdom in the Ile de France, and both Louis's baronage and Henry II were unruly and untrustworthy. The French king's own position was precarious because most of his great vassals in Normandy, Gascony and elsewhere were only nominally subject to the French monarch and in practice behaved as independent potentates. This was an era of shifting loyalties where, in tentative movements towards central government, self-interest prevailed over morality, where states and frontiers might be decided over drunken brawls, and personal affronts determine decisions of public policy.

In the kaleidoscopic pattern of twelfth century medieval Europe few countries other than England had centralised government, the absence of which weakened the position of those rulers who needed to make quick and decisive decisions. The French king suffered from this structural weakness in his government which undermined his ability to provide Becket with greater support. Indeed, as Fisher points out "... there resulted a chronic state of hostility between the kings of England and France which lasted with some intermissions until the middle of the fifteenth century". [43]

The logical prop to the archbishop's position should have been the pope; but as we have seen, Alexander himself had difficulties with the Holy Roman Empire and was always conscious of the dangers of an alliance between the emperor and Henry II.

Despite this, as noted earlier, the pope displayed indecision in dealing with Henry at critical moments. Had he imposed an interdict or excommunication much earlier he might well have brought the king to heel before the murder. The pope was certainly capable of resolution as he demonstrated in 1177, after Becket's death, when his diplomacy prevented an English alliance with Barbarossa.

While it is clear that Alexander found Becket tiresome on occasions because he would not compromise, he was also well aware that the archbishop was a loyal and trusted cleric and an essential support for the pope when Alexander was threatened by the emperor.

Barbarossa was the European bogeyman in this narrative, whose periodic military appearances south of the Alps concentrated thoughts and tested alliances. Recalcitrant children in the towns and countryside of Piedmont and Lombardy would, no doubt, be warned by their exhausted nurse or mother, at the end of a long day, "If you are a bad boy then 'Barbar' will get you", as other European children would be warned about 'Boney' more than five and a half centuries into the future.

We may also speculate that, had military resistance to the emperor from the Lombard League been both earlier and successful the denouement for Becket could well have been different; but that was not to be.

Of course, historians have differed widely in their assessments of Becket's character and performance. John Guy is broadly sympathetic towards the primate in his struggle with the king, whom he portrays as treacherous, while he considers that Becket represented the forces of reason and decency against tyranny.

However, A.L. Poole is more censorious of the archbishop since, while acknowledging that "he had certain virtues: he led a pure life in an age when chastity, especially at court, was lax, and he was of a generous disposition", the historian goes on to declare that "looked at dispassionately, however, he appears as a vain, obstinate, and ambitious man who sought always to keep himself in the public eye; he was above all a man of extremes, a man who knew no half measures", and who was a great actor playing a role in the theatre of ambition. Guy echoes Poole's assessment of the actor playing to the audience, and Thomas Becket was undoubtedly a man of vaunting ambition, while his youthful displays of opulence and splendour were indecorous; but throughout his life he remained true to his friends and beliefs.

In many ways it is easier to admire Becket than to love him, but numerous 'saintly' men [44] had early careers which were less than admirable, while Becket throughout demonstrated intense loyalty to his employer whether he be Theobald, Henry or Alexander. In that respect he resembled a dog, unconditionally faithful to its master.

The final and psychological question relates to the nature of Becket's martyrdom. In that respect Poole's assessment of Becket as a man of ambition and intransigence who was "a great actor superbly living the parts he was called upon to play", leading him to a form of contrived martyrdom, is a judgment which may be somewhat harsh, but which still appears to contain an element of veracity; since so much of his career seems to have been plotted out, like a contemporary politician assiduously parading his self-perceived virtues through the corridors and milieu of Westminster, ceaselessly grasping the hand of anyone who might assist his advancement.

Poole quotes EA Freeman in comparing Becket with Saint Anselm [45] where Freeman writes that Becket "had a theory of what a saint ought to do, while Anselm was a saint naturally without thinking about it". [46] Poole comments: "This is true of Becket's whole career; there was an element of artificiality in it all".

The nature of Becket's martyrdom has echoes in twentieth century Dublin when the poet and schoolmaster, Padraic Pearse, led the doomed Easter uprising on the twenty third of April 1916. The two men had certain common characteristics in that both were overtly theatrical, single men, close to their mothers and (certainly in the case of Pearse) uncomfortable with other women. John Guy, in writing about Becket's sexuality, leaves open the nature of his relationship with Richer de L'Aigle, but states that the mature man could not have been homosexual because this would have been exposed following his break with Henry.

Pearse's biographer, Ruth Dudley Edwards, [47] considers that he "would not be the first or last brilliant schoolmaster whose ability to understand, inspire and relate to his pupils was rooted in both arrested emotional development and homoeroticism". It is possibly the case that both men were examples of repressed homoeroticism.

But what links them above all is that they each WANTED death, and they longed for it – for a cause: Becket for his church and religion, Pearse for his country and liberty. After the failure of the uprising Pearse was sentenced to be executed, at the subsequent court martial. Therefore, as Dudley Edwards writes: "He was ensuring he was given the death sentence he craved". As he expressed it in a letter written to his mother from Killmainham Jail the night before his execution, "This is the death I should have asked for if God had given me the choice of all deaths – to die a soldier's death for Ireland and for freedom. We have done right".

The archbishop expressed his wish by action (or rather, inaction) when refusing to deny his murderers access to the cathedral; and perhaps the last words should therefore, belong to Thomas Becket, as imagined by Eliot. [48]

"The last temptation is the greatest treason:
To do the right deed for the wrong reason."

Genealogical Table
The Normans and Angevins

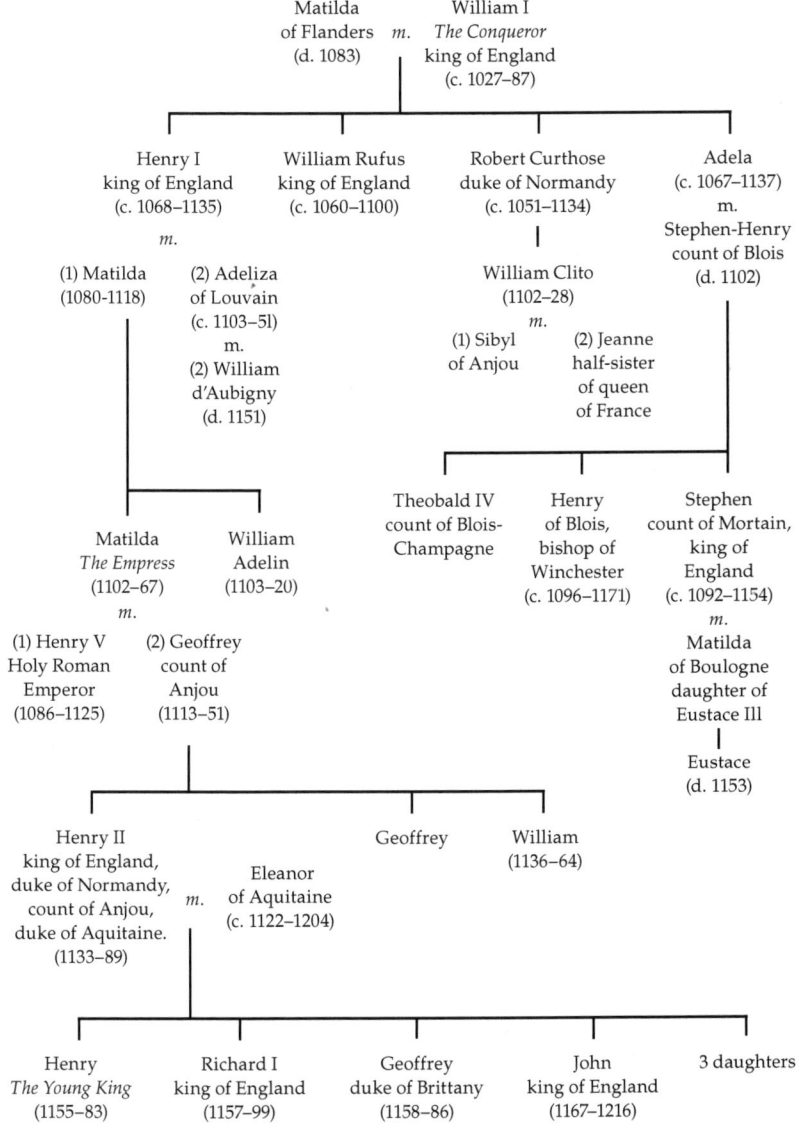

Matilda of Flanders (d. 1083) *m.* William I *The Conqueror* king of England (c. 1027–87)

Henry I king of England (c. 1068–1135) *m.*

William Rufus king of England (c. 1060–1100)

Robert Curthose duke of Normandy (c. 1051–1134)

Adela (c. 1067–1137) m. Stephen-Henry count of Blois (d. 1102)

(1) Matilda (1080-1118)

(2) Adeliza of Louvain (c. 1103–5l) m. (2) William d'Aubigny (d. 1151)

William Clito (1102–28) *m.*

(1) Sibyl of Anjou

(2) Jeanne half-sister of queen of France

Theobald IV count of Blois-Champagne

Henry of Blois, bishop of Winchester (c. 1096–1171)

Stephen count of Mortain, king of England (c. 1092–1154) *m.* Matilda of Boulogne daughter of Eustace Ill

Eustace (d. 1153)

Matilda *The Empress* (1102–67) *m.*

William Adelin (1103–20)

(1) Henry V Holy Roman Emperor (1086–1125)

(2) Geoffrey count of Anjou (1113–51)

Henry II king of England, duke of Normandy, count of Anjou, duke of Aquitaine. (1133–89) *m.*

Eleanor of Aquitaine (c. 1122–1204)

Geoffrey

William (1136–64)

Henry *The Young King* (1155–83)

Richard I king of England (1157–99)

Geoffrey duke of Brittany (1158–86)

John king of England (1167–1216)

3 daughters

NOTES

1. HAL Fisher: *A History of Europe.*

2. In fact the Emperor Honorius had moved the capital of the Western Roman Empire from Rome to Ravenna in 402 partly for defensive reasons – it was surrounded by marshes – and also because the port had excellent maritime routes to the Eastern Empire. Ravenna remained the capital until 476 when the empire collapsed and it became the capital of the Kingdom of the Ostrogoths – until 540 when it was re-conquered by the Eastern Roman (Byzantine) Empire and was the centre of the Byzantine Exarchate (a Byzantine province governed by an exarch who was a viceroy of the Byzantine emperor) of Ravenna. Subsequently the Franks invaded in 751 after which it emerged as the seat of the kingdom of the Lombards.

3. *Guelf* is the Italian form of "Welf" which was used as a war-cry at the battle of Weinsberg in 1140 by the followers of Welf VI of Bavaria; while *Ghibelline* is the Italian form of "Waiblingen", a town in Wurtemberg, part of the possessions of the Hohenstaufen emperor Conrad III, which was shouted by his followers in the same battle.

4. Had Carlyle been a man of the twenty first century he would no doubt, on considering Eleanor, have included the words "and Great Women".

5. He was Nicholas Breakspear who, as Hadrian or Adrian IV, became the only English pope.

6. A Margravate was a mark, frontier or border province of medieval Germany, and its governor was a Margrave. In the twelfth century the office became hereditary. A Landgraviate was a large territory in medieval Central Germany and its governor was a Landgrave. The office and title were hereditary.

7. Duke of Saxony 1142–80 and Duke of Bavaria 1156–80.

8. Henry the Lion had recovered Saxony from Conrad in 1142.

9. Subsequently, in 1174, Henry failed to support his sovereign with reinforcements in another Italian campaign. Partly as a result of this Frederick was soundly beaten at the battle of Legnano. In revenge the Emperor, in 1180, had Henry stripped of his lands and, in 1182 he was sent into exile.

10. The title 'Holy' Roman Emperor was not in fact used until 1254.

11. Members of the League included, inter alia, Verona, Milan, Padua, Venice, Bologna, Parma and Vicenza.

12. Barbarossa was in fact crowned by Adrian IV in 1155, Eugenius having died in 1153.

13. Roger II (1095–1154) was a descendant of the Northmen (or Vikings) who had migrated from Scandinavia and settled in what became known as Normandy during the early part of the tenth century. They embraced Christianity and other facets of Latin society and, coming to be called Normans, they combined firm government with military powers and social sophistication. This conjunction of talents created a duchy, which had emerged by the middle of the eleventh century, as one of the most powerful states in Western Europe.

By the beginning of the eleventh century, many Normans had moved south from Normandy to southern Italy and in 1130 Roger II, who was an expansionist by inclination, was crowned king of Sicily by the anti-pope Anacletus II. The new monarch had already obtained general recognition as Duke of Benevento (from 1128) and of Apulia (from 1129) and by 1130 was master of all southern Italy.

This speedy expansionism northward took Roger's fiefdom to the southern border of the Papal States, a course of events which sounded numerous alarms in the Lateran. The pope was therefore, potentially threatened by the Holy Roman Empire from the north and by the kingdom of Sicily from the south. In order to minimize the risk Pope Innocent II (1130–1143) had wanted the Principality of Capua to be independent and act as a buffer state between the Kingdom of Sicily and the Papal States. However Roger had rejected this proposal, and in doing so, provoked further papal suspicion as to the Norman intentions, a suspicion which was validated when war erupted in 1130 and lasted for ten years.

14. This was the precursor to the Great Schism of the fourteenth century which lasted from 1378 to 1417, during which the anti-popes resided at Avignon.

15. This is still the position today.

16. They were Urban II in 1095–6, Paschal II in 1106–7, Gelasius II in 1118–19, Calixtus II in 1119–20, Innocent II in 1130–2, Eugenius III in 1147–8 and Alexander III in 1162–5. As LS Robinson points out in his book *The Papacy 1073–1198: Continuity and Innovation* "Only after the end of the Alexandrine Schism and the return to Rome negotiated by Clement III (1188) did the popes cease to rely on their refuge in France".

17. This castle was originally built on the orders of the English king, William II to defend the Vexin County area of Normandy from the French king's threatened acquisition.

18. Henry, and his sons Richard 1 and John, who between them ruled from 1154 to 1216, were also known as the Angevins, being from Anjou, until the loss of Anjou to the French during John's reign.

19. Thus the English and German allies were each led by auburn monarchs.

20. In contrast to the French kings who were constantly striving to assert control over powerful nobles in their semi-independent fiefdoms.

21. Scutage or 'shield money' was in effect a tax imposed on the king's knights in substitution for the feudal obligation of the knights with their followers to serve in the royal army.

22. As Henry II was still alive this was unique in England but common practice on the continent as a way of securing the succession.

23. Their mid twentieth century congeners may well have been the USA President, John Kennedy, and his wife, Jackie. Admittedly their 'Court' was founded on Camelot rather than Poitiers, but in each case there was the entwining of brilliance with beauty, action with glamour, the reverence for courtly love with emotional instability, public successes with private failure, and international achievement with personal tragedy.

24. Steven Runciman in *A History of the Crusades*, suggests the Germans numbered nearly 20,000 including pilgrims, with the French a little smaller perhaps about 18,000. However Alison Weir in *Eleanor of Aquitaine* states the French army "numbered around 100,000 persons". and invokes John of Salisbury in his work *Historia Pontificalis*.

25. This represented about twice England's annual revenue.

26. There is some confusion over Thomas Becket's surname: The Dictionary of National Biography, first published between 1885 and 1901, refers to him as 'Thomas a Becket' but admits that three contemporary sources refer to just 'Becket' and that the future archbishop always called himself 'Thomas of London'. There appears to be no evidence that the name 'Thomas a Becket' was used in his lifetime, and it has been suggested that this was a post-Reformation usage influenced by the example of the scholar and divine, Thomas a Kempis, whose work, *The Imitation of Christ*, was widely admired in the late Middle Ages. The author wonders whether it was considered that a 'French' style of address would be somewhat more fitting for such a popular saint of French origin.

27. But, whatever the explanation, it seems that modern scholarship prefers the use of the title 'Thomas Becket'.

28. John of Salisbury was one of the great theologians and scholars of his age and became Bishop of Chartres. He was present in Canterbury cathedral at the time of the murder.

29. AL Poole in *Domesday Book to Magna Carta*.

30. In fact this became academic since Eustace died in 1153, the year before Henry II succeeded to the throne in 1154.

31. Knowledge of this undoubtedly influenced Becket's decisions as archbishop in his future dealings with Henry II.

32. Also known as the Treaty of Winchester or Westminster.

33. Becket's appointments were secular in nature rather than clerical and he was not ordained a priest until 2nd June 1162, the day before his consecration as archbishop.

34. The county of Vexin, on a fertile plain in north west France, and bounded by the Seine on its southern side, was essential to the English monarch to protect the north east frontier of Normandy

35. e.g. at the council of Woodstock held on the 1st July 1163 the king proposed that the sheriffs' fees for raising the royal revenue and the costs of local administration should no longer be deductible by the sheriffs from the money raised but all should be handed over to the national exchequer. Becket opposed this and said that if the king persisted with his proposal the church would refuse to pay any such money.

36. On 23rd September 1162 Henry and Louis VII of France had met Alexander at Coucy-sur-Loire where the two kings recognised him as the legitimate pope against the claims of Paschal III.

37. Excommunication in the Roman Catholic church at this time was an ecclesiastical punishment which prohibited an individual or even a whole nation from receiving the sacraments and, in some cases, from attending the communion service; in the case of an excommunicated priest, he was forbidden from administering the sacraments.

38. i.e, in Gaeta, Benevento, Anagni and Venice.

39. An interdict was an ecclesiastical punishment in the Catholic church imposed upon an individual, place or area, restricting or forbidding participation in or performance of, selected services or sacraments.

40. However, Alison Weir contends (in her book *Eleanor of Aquitaine*) that

"Henry had decided not to have her crowned with her husband at that stage because he believed that to do so in the face of archiepiscopal prohibition might offend Louis more than if she was not crowned at all." This seems unlikely since Henry had every opportunity to advise Louis had he wished, and in any event pope Alexander was the final arbitrator. and would surely have been consulted by Henry had he considered the matter.

41. For long periods their numbers have exceeded those seeking the sanctuaries of Assisi or Santiago de Compostela.

42. In 1538 Thomas Becket's shrine was desecrated and demolished on the orders of King Henry VIII.

43. In *Eleanor of Aquitaine.*

44. HAL Fisher in *A History of Europe.*

45. Saint Paul is an obvious example.

46. Archbishop of Canterbury 1093–1109, who was canonised in c1163.

47. E.A. Freeman, (1823–1892, historian and Liberal politician) in a letter to Dean Hook, *Life and Letters of E.A. Freeman* ed. by W. R. Stephens.

48. In her book *The Seven.*

49. In T.S. Eliot's play, *Murder in the Cathedral*

A Brief Bibliography

I wish to acknowledge that in preparing this book, I have consulted at length the following works:

Ruth Dudley Edwards - *The Seven*

T.S. Eliot - *Murder in the Cathedral*

H.A.L. Fisher – *A History of Europe*

John Guy – *Thomas Becket*

Amy Kelly - *Eleanor of Aquitaine*

A.L. Poole – *Domesday Book to Magna Carta*

Steven Runciman – *A History of the Crusades*

(Ed. By W. R. Stephens) – *Life and Letters of E. A. Freeman*

Alison Weir – *Eleanor of Aquitaine*

About the Author

William Moyle worked as a lawyer and loves history, literature, poetry, music and cricket. He and his wife have lived in Herefordshire for seventeen years and were among those instrumental in setting up the Friends of St. Thomas à Becket Church. In 2016 William was asked by the Friends to research their patron saint and this book is the result. The writer's own Holy Trinity is Schubert, WB Yeats and leg-spin bowling.

Image Credits